The Wonderful Water Cycle

Contents

Rigby

A Harcourt Achieve Imprint

www.Rigby.com

1-800-531-5015

Water

Hi! I'm a drop of water. I can go many places. I can help fill oceans, lakes, and rivers. I can fight fires, and I can water gardens. I can even be in your water glass!

Did you know that Earth has always had the same amount of water on it? The water you swim in, wash with, and drink has been used over and over. Water moves in a never-ending circle called the water cycle. Come with me, and I'll show you how it works.

How Water Changes

Right now I am a liquid. I flow and splash and can get things wet. You can pour me and drink me. Watch me flow out of this cup.

But I don't always have to be a liquid. I can also be a gas, like the air. Or, I can be solid as a rock. These are my three states of matter: solid, liquid, and gas.

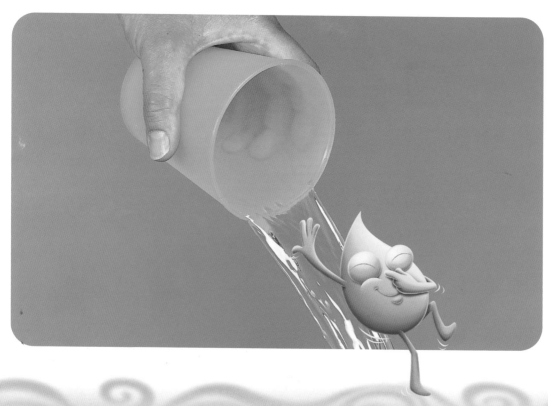

When the sun warms me, I evaporate. This means I change into a gas called water vapor and go into the air. Then you can't see me anymore. Let's see how this works.

Try It!

Here is something you can try at home.

1. In the morning, put a teaspoon of water in a dish.

2. Carefully put the dish in the warm sun.

3. Late in the afternoon, check how much water is left in the dish.

What happened to the water? Where did it go? Heat from the sun made the water evaporate into the air! Now it's water vapor. This happens even on cloudy days because the sun is always heating the earth.

How Water Changes Again

After I turn into water vapor, I ride on the wind. I travel across the land and the oceans to many new places. You can feel me on your face as I blow with the breeze. The wind also carries me high up into the sky.

When water vapor gets very high, it starts to get colder. As the vapor gets colder, it begins to condense. This means that the water vapor changes from a gas back into a liquid. It changes into tiny drops of water.

These drops gather together to make clouds. It takes billions and billions of water drops to make a cloud. The more water drops in a cloud, the darker the cloud looks. After a while, the clouds get so heavy with water that the drops start to fall from the sky as rain.

Try This!

You can make water vapor change into water. It's really easy!

1. First fill a tall glass with ice.

2. Next add water to the glass that is filled with ice.

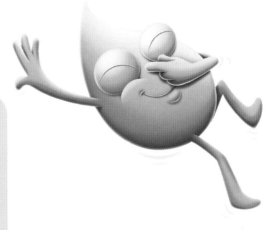

3. Now watch the outside of the glass. What do you think will happen?

Touch the glass with your finger. What does it feel like? As the air next to the glass gets colder, the outside of the glass gets wet. The water vapor in the air is condensing on the glass.

Rain and Snow

When clouds get filled with lots of water, they become big and heavy. Then the drops fall to Earth as rain.

If the air is cold enough, some of the drops in the clouds will freeze into snow. When the snow melts, it becomes water again.

The Water Cycle

Water returns to Earth as rain or snow. It splashes into oceans, lakes, and rivers. It falls onto the ground and sometimes makes puddles. Water goes into streams and rivers that carry it to the ocean.

water condenses

rain

river